THE PONY EXPRESS

Heroes in the Saddle

Moments in History

by Shirley Jordan

Perfection Learning®

About the Author

Shirley Jordan is a retired elementary school teacher and principal. Currently a lecturer in the teacher-training program at California State University, Fullerton, California, she sees exciting things happening in the world of social studies. Shirley loves to travel—with a preference for sites important to U.S. history.

She has had more than 50 travel articles published in recent years. It was through her travels that she became interested in "moments in history," those ironic and little-known stories that make one exclaim, "I didn't know that!" Such stories are woven throughout her books.

Image Credits: St. Joseph Museum, St. Joseph, Missouri pp. 9, 18, 21, 22, 36, 47; Bettmann/Corbis pp. 41, 45; David G. Houser/Corbis p. 44; Jonathon Blair/Corbis p. 8; Wells Fargo Bank p. 24

Pony Express Museum, St. Joseph, Missouri p. 2; Library of Congress pp. 7, 25, 28, 40, 54; Digital Stock p. 27; Corel cover art, pp. 32, 48, 49; Federal Reserve Bank of San Francisco p. 43. Some images copyright www.arttoday.com.

Cover Photographs: Pony Express riders from left to right: Johnny Fry, who rode the first leg of the first westbound Pony Express run; John Burnett, who later worked as a Wells Fargo agent; Richard Erastus Egan, who survived many close calls to become a bishop of his church; Jack Keetley, who rode 24 hours nonstop

Book Design: Alan D. Stanley

Table of Contents

Timeline of Important Events

January 1860	Senator Gwin of California meets William Russell in Washington, D.C. They talk about ways to speed mail between the eastern states and California.
January 27, 1860	William Russell sends a telegram to his son, John. It says William Russell will establish a Pony Express by April 3.
February 4, 1860	William Russell hurries back to Leavenworth, Kansas, to meet with his partners, Majors and Waddell. They do not like the idea of the Pony Express. But Russell has given his promise to Senator Gwin. The partners decide to go along with the plan.
April 3, 1860	The first Pony Express deliveries start out from St. Joseph, Missouri, and San Francisco, California.
April 13, 1860	The first *mochila* of mail from St. Joseph reaches Sacramento, California. From there the letters will travel by boat to San Francisco.

The first Pony Express mail packet from California arrives in St. Joseph. |

4

May 7, 1860	Five men are killed by Indians at the Pyramid Lake station. Trouble with the Indians grows.
May 31, 1860	The Pony Express stops its service for three weeks.
Late June 1860	Service begins again. Now there are two deliveries per week.
December 1860	William Russell is arrested and accused of taking bonds belonging to the Indians.
February 1861	The Pony Express is merged with the Butterfield-Wells Fargo Company.
April 1861	The Civil War breaks out.
July 1861	Work begins on the transcontinental telegraph.
October 24, 1861	The first telegraphed message travels across the country from San Francisco to Washington, D.C.
October 26, 1861	The Pony Express comes to an end.

Introduction

It was the middle of the 1800s. Cities in America's eastern states had grown larger and larger. But crowding was not for everyone. Hundreds of brave men and women wanted open land. So they packed up and headed west to make a new life.

Then, in 1849, came another reason to move west. Gold was discovered in California. Thousands of Americans traveled across the United States to seek that gold. A few found it. Most did not.

In 1850, this rush to find gold filled California with 100,000 new citizens.

But those who went west gave up something important to them. There was no regular mail service from town to town. And the telegraph reached only as far west as St. Joseph, Missouri.

Even more alarming, there was talk of a civil war. Northerners and Southerners argued loudly in Congress. Each month the risk of war grew. But news of these events was endlessly slow to reach California.

As time passed, the settlers in the West felt more and more cut off from the rest of the country.

1
Chapter

A New Plan Is Needed

Senator William Gwin paced the floor of his Washington, D.C., office. It was a day in late 1859. Californians had chosen him to represent them. It was his job to tell the government what Californians needed.

The senator knew what the people wanted. They wanted to send letters to family members back east. And they wanted news and letters in return.

Gwin was a member of the United States Committee on the Post Offices. But there seemed so little he could do for the people of his state. If only there were a better way to move the mail. It would have to be fast and dependable.

Senator William Gwin

Much of the mail moved by sea in 1859. Letters mailed in New York started out for California on steamships. They traveled down the east coast of North America to Panama. From there, it was less than 40 miles across the *isthmus*, a stretch of land between the oceans.

At first, mules shuffled along these miles. They carried the mail in large saddlebags. Finally in 1855, a railroad line had been built across the isthmus.

On the Pacific Ocean side, another ship picked up the mail sacks. It carried them north to San Francisco. From there the mail was delivered to other towns by wagon.

Even the fastest mail coming through Panama took three weeks. And if a settler lived a great distance from San Francisco, letters might not arrive for two or three more weeks.

A few companies carried mail by land. The government paid them to move it by stagecoach across the vast plains of the West. The most successful of these was the Butterfield Overland Mail Company.

But the Butterfield route dipped far south to avoid the cruel winters. And this added 800 miles to the trip. A letter carried by Butterfield stagecoach took at least 23 days to reach California. And outlaws often held up the stages and stole the mail.

As Senator Gwin paced, he thought. Maybe just one man, riding alone, could solve the problem. Maybe such a man could head *straight* across the country. He could leave St. Joseph, where the eastern railroad ended. When he was tired, he could pass the mail to another horse and rider. More riders could form a relay. It could continue west, all the way to Sacramento. From there a boat could easily sail on to San Francisco.

William Russell

This idea of a relay on horseback was not a new one. It had been used hundreds of years before. Military messages had been relayed in Persia, Rome, and ancient China.

But who could make his idea a success? Senator Gwin knew just the man. He would talk to William Russell.

Russell was a man who liked to try new things. He had helped found the growing town of Denver. And he had started a stagecoach line to the West.

Now Russell and his two partners ran a company carrying freight between St. Joseph and Salt Lake City, Utah. Their company hauled wagon loads of supplies from the East to the settlers and miners in the West.

Alexander Majors

Senator Gwin also knew Russell's two partners, Alexander Majors and William Waddell. They were very careful men. Those two did not like to take chances. Majors, a bookkeeper, guarded the company's money. Waddell knew the western plains well. He was an expert on weather and Indian affairs. And he was a well-respected descendant of the famous Pilgrim governor, William Bradford.

William Waddell

In January 1860, Gwin went to William Russell. He shared his idea of a relay of riders to carry the mail. Right away, Russell was excited.

"I'll talk to my partners," he promised. "It would be a fine new business for our company."

But Majors and Waddell were slow to approve of the new idea.

"How would we pay for such a thing?" asked Majors. "It will cost us a fortune just to start such a business."

"And what about the Indians?" asked Waddell. "A route directly west would send a rider right through the middle of tribal lands."

Majors spoke again. "And there'd be bandits too. How can we be sure the horse and rider would be safe?"

Russell didn't want to hear such talk. He was in a hurry! He would call the business the Pony Express. He wanted to begin the relay route in just two months. And he proposed that a letter would travel across the country in ten days.

His partners were stunned.

"Ten days!" cried Alexander Majors. "How can that be?"

"It would take twice that long," said Waddell. "And what would we do if snow closes the trail?"

"A man on a horse can make good time. Better than any stagecoach," said Russell. "We'll have day riders and night riders. I figure a letter can go from St. Joseph to Salt Lake City in four days. After that, we have six more days to take it over the mountains into California."

Russell would listen to no arguments. If Majors and Waddell weren't interested, he would start the Pony Express by himself.

The two younger partners thought for a long time. Finally, they decided to join Russell in this new plan. Maybe they could make the Pony Express a success. Then they surely would get a fine government contract.

Plans began at once. Russell, Majors, and Waddell set the best employees of their freight company to work.

Chapter 2

Preparing the Route

Russell's company already had a number of stagecoach stations along the route west. Some of these could be made bigger and used as home stations. A Pony Express rider could rest there until his next turn to move the mail.

In addition to 25 home stations, the Pony Express would need 165 swing stations. Here a rider would stop for just two minutes to change to a fresh horse.

The distance between swing stations was decided by the number of miles a horse could run at full speed. The stations would be ten miles apart where the trail was rugged. And where the trail was flat, they would be twice that far apart.

If there was water at the swing station, fine. If not, it would be brought in along with food, grain, and other supplies.

The new Pony Express route stretched for 1,840 miles. It roughly followed the old Oregon Trail. That had been used by the early settlers 50 years before.

The stations differed greatly. At the west end was Sacramento. And in the east was St. Joseph. Forests were common in both places. It was easy to build the station houses of timber. But in Nebraska, crews had to put together sod huts. On long desert stretches, adobe was the building material.

Sometimes the land was truly barren. Then the crews had to dig a cave in a hillside. They added a roof of logs. These were hauled from a wooded area many miles away.

Each swing station housed a station keeper. And he had one or two helpers to take care of the horses.

The home stations were not much larger. A rider waiting for his next turn had a shelter with rough bunks and a few pieces of simple kitchen equipment.

But the home stations had better food. The company saw that supplies were delivered each week. Popular foods included bacon, beans, cheese, and flour for biscuits. And at most home stations, a hunter was paid to supply fresh meat.

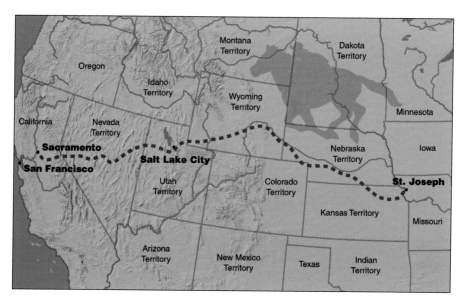

Chapter

Choosing the Riders

Early in 1860, posters appeared in towns and cities between St. Joseph and Sacramento. The message was repeated in the newspapers of San Francisco, Salt Lake City, and St. Joseph. It read

WANTED

YOUNG, SKINNY,
WIRY FELLOWS NOT
OVER EIGHTEEN. MUST BE
EXPERT RIDERS WILLING
TO RISK DEATH DAILY.
ORPHANS PREFERRED.
WAGES $25 PER WEEK.

Hundreds of young men were looking for adventure. They rushed to apply. How exciting it would be to ride for the Pony Express!

The company chose 80 riders. Here is a letter that could have been written by one of those young men.

Sacramento, California
March 20, 1860

Dear Ma,
    I hope the stagecoach will soon get this letter to you there in St. Joseph.
    By the time you read this, I will have an exciting new job. It's with a new business called the Pony Express. (But it really uses horses, not ponies.)
    There are no stagecoaches. Just horses. And the Pony Express won't carry anything but mail. Only one rider and one horse at a time. We're to relay the mail between home stations. The company plans to move a letter from here in Sacramento to back there in St. Joseph in only ten days!
    You will be proud of me, I think. A whole passel of riders tried out for the jobs. They say more than 200. I was one of the 80 hired. We start riding April 3.
    Chasing buffalo across the plains made me a good rider, I guess. That's what the company wanted. It also helped that I could use a compass. And I could follow a trail. I was under 18 too. (But they did hire some older men.) Best of all, the man who hired me seemed glad I could shoot straight.
    I don't know what stretch of the route I'll be riding yet. The horses here at the western end are 200 top-quality mustangs. I hear some of them are half wild. But that's OK because such horses are mighty fast. And strong. Strong enough to pick their way over the high mountain passes in the Sierra Nevada. Especially in the winter.

The horses on the eastern end of the route will be fast ones too. The company bought 300 thoroughbreds for that part. They are the best mares money can buy. Most of them came from the army. They always have the best horseflesh on the plains.

Thoroughbred mares can't climb trails as well as mustangs. So they wouldn't do well out here in the mountains. But they're the fastest horses alive on the flat, open trail.

Ma, you won't believe what the company is paying for this horseflesh. Two hundred dollars an animal! That's four times the going price! I just can't wait to ride such animals.

And they'll all be grain-fed. Indian ponies eat range grass. That's why they're slower and get tired. Having a grain-fed horse can save a man's life if he has to make a run for it.

And you should see our saddles, Ma. The company is having them specially made by the Landis Company in St. Louis. They're the finest leather. But they're light as a feather.

The letters we carry will be in a mochila. That's a thin leather blanket with four pockets that can be locked up. The mochila fits right over the saddle. We can throw it to the next rider in less than a minute.

We'll each carry two Colt revolvers, a knife, and a carbine rifle. We also get a horn to blow when we come near the next station. And, oh yes. Mr. Russell, the oldest partner in the company, has given us each a Bible to carry.

This Mr. Russell has a rule. All his riders have to sign a pledge. The pledge says we will never use bad language, never quarrel with the other riders, and will always act honestly. I guess Mr. Russell likes things done the same way you do. That's how you tried to raise me, Ma.

The company prefers to hire orphans. The newspaper ad said that. But I was lucky. The company man who talked to me said you lived far away. So it was almost like I didn't have any kin.

Do you remember how you always wanted to fatten me up? How you pushed me to eat your good cooking? Well, I'm glad it didn't work. The company won't hire anyone over 130 pounds.

The Pony Express has another rule. But this one's not written down. At least I don't think it is. It's something they keep saying to us. It tells us what's important.

MAIL FIRST. HORSE SECOND. SELF LAST.

I'll send you some money soon, Ma. We're to get $25 a week. That sure is better then the $30 a month I got as a cowhand last year.

I hope you aim to write to me. Just think. Before long, you can send a letter by Pony Express. And it will get to me in ten days. Not 23 days like the Butterfield Express. Not a month like the mail across Panama.

But Pony Express letters do cost a bit more than those slower ways. The charge is $5 a half ounce. So write small, and use tissue paper to keep the weight down.

> Your loving son,
> Buddy

Chapter 4

Only the Best Equipment

The Pony Express owners, Russell, Majors, and Waddell, had spent a great deal of money. Many new stations were finished. The company's horses were the best money could buy. And horses like that did not graze on prairie grass. The feed they ate was expensive. Wagons brought the feed and water from long distances.

Special saddles were made for the Pony Express too. Some historians say they were designed by one of the riders, W. A. Cates. Such a saddle weighed only 13 pounds. Saddles used by other western riders weighed three times that much. With such light saddles and light riders, a horse could run its top speed easily.

A light leather rectangle called a *mochila* went over the saddle. (In Spanish that word means "knapsack.") At each corner of the mochila was a mail pouch called a *cantina*. Three of the cantinas were locked with keys held by the Pony Express owners. The fourth one could be opened with the key kept by any stationmaster. This way, letters could be added at stations along the way. The time cards for the riders were in that fourth cantina too.

It was easy for a rider to yank the mochila from his saddle and throw it across a fresh horse. Such an exchange took no more than one or two minutes.

Chapter

The Big Day Arrives

It was early afternoon on April 3, 1860, in St. Joseph. A long-awaited day had come.

The crowd grew. It was a Tuesday. But most stores in St. Joseph had shut down for the big event. Men, women, and children pressed closer.

A brass band played. The crowd cheered them on as they offered "Yankee Doodle" and "Turkey in the Straw." In between songs, there were speeches from the town leaders.

Johnny Fry leaned against the railroad ticket office in the shade. He was 23. And he was a handsome young man with suntanned skin. Groups of young women looked his way, then giggled. It was clear they liked his looks.

Fry's eyes darted over the crowd. Then he leaned forward to peer down the railroad track. The mail train from Washington, D.C., had been due at 4:00. It was past that time now.

"Hey, Johnny," a friend called. "How do you feel?"

"Ready to go," Fry grumbled. "I've been ready to mount up and ride ever since my name was drawn. I like being first to leave from St. Jo. But I sure wish that train would come with my letters."

Johnny Fry was proud of his new job. He had been one of the first men hired to ride for the Pony Express. Today was his big day.

He was not a large man. At 5 feet 6 inches tall, he weighed 125 pounds. Alexander Majors had set the weight limit at 130.

"There's no need to overload such fine horses," he'd said.

Both rider and pony were decked out for the big day. Fry wore a red flannel shirt, blue pants, and a decorated kerchief around his neck. His boots were expensive. His jacket was of fine buckskin. A huge sombrero shaded his face. These fancy clothes were the idea of William Russell. He wanted to make a show with his new company.

The fine mare Fry was to ride had been combed and curried. She was a high-spirited horse. And she had caught the excitement of the day.

But alas for the young horse, the crowd refused to leave her alone. Tired of waiting for the mail train from Washington, the men and women grew restless. Soon a few people had plucked hairs from the animal's tail. A fine souvenir of the day, they thought.

Others joined in. Before long the horse's mane and tail were growing thin. And her good temper was gone. She stomped and pawed the ground.

Still Johnny Fry looked down the track. The special mail train was more than two hours late.

At last, at 6:30, the train arrived. A loaded cannon was ready at the station. It boomed a welcome as the train pulled in. A cheer went up from the crowd.

The train was pulled by a wood-burning locomotive. It had stopped several times to pick up a new supply of fuel. The time had grown later and later.

As soon as the Pony Express mail was unloaded, it was packed into the leather mochila. On this first run, the riders would carry 49 letters. They had been written on tissue paper to keep the

cost down. With the letters were five private telegrams and a copy of the St. Joseph *Daily Gazette*. It had been specially printed on tissue paper.

All were stuffed into an oiled silk packet to protect them from rain. Altogether, they weighed less than 15 pounds.

Fry tucked several hard navy biscuits into his pockets. He added some cooked bacon wrapped in newspaper.

Quickly, he swung the mochila over his saddle. He grabbed a canteen of cold tea. Mounting, he turned the animal's head toward the nearby ferry. His ride would actually begin on the other side of the Missouri River.

The horse's hooves clomped onto the waiting boat, the *Dover*. The ferryman, Captain Blackinstone, nodded to Fry in relief. He, too, had waited hours for the historic ride to begin. By now it was 7:15. The paddle wheel began to turn.

It was a short trip across the water. Just enough time for Fry to change out of the fancy riding clothes. He put on an old, soft shirt and dungarees he liked better.

21

As the ferryboat reached shore, man and horse were ready to leave. A crowd parted to make room. In a moment, Johnny Fry was galloping down the road on his Pony Express route. His ride would be 40 miles long.

It took Fry eight hours to reach his home station. During this time, he changed horses three times. At each relay station, trainers had his fresh horse waiting. Each was prancing and ready to go.

It was still dark when Fry rode into Granada, Kansas, the end of his run. He had managed to make up 30 minutes of the time he had lost waiting for the train.

Standing in the doorway was Don Rising, the next rider. The 16-year-old was anxious to be on his way. Quickly, he caught the mochila as Fry sailed it to him. He tucked it over his saddle and mounted. With a wave, he spurred his horse.

And so the relay had begun. The Pony Express was rushing mail to the West.

Chapter 6

Setting Out from the West

Hundreds of people in St. Joseph had waited for the tardy mail train. At the same time, another crowd gathered in San Francisco.

The Pony Express was to deliver mail between St. Joseph and San Francisco. It would travel both east and west. But at the San Francisco end there was a difference.

Once the Pony Express began its regular delivery, no horse and rider would travel between San Francisco and Sacramento. A boat could more easily make that trip. Each week, a paddle wheeler would take the San Francisco mail to Sacramento. Then the Pony Express rider would travel east with it from there.

But this was the first day. It was the very first trip from west to east. The crowd at San Francisco wanted to be part of the excitement.

Everyone loved the idea of the Pony Express. Some in the crowd had already begun to shorten its name to just "the Pony."

The fine saddles ordered by the company had not yet reached California. The specially-designed mochila had not arrived, either. For now, the mail would be carried in ordinary saddlebags. On the side they said "Overland Pony Express."

A band played. And there were fireworks and flowers. A small yellow-brown horse decorated with flags and bells pawed the ground.

This little horse would only work for the Pony Express that one day. She would carry the San Francisco letters from the telegraph office to the paddle wheeler, the *Antelope.*

The rider for this short trip was James Randall. Like the little yellow mare, Randall was to ride for the company only this one time. And that might have been a good thing.

As Randall prepared to start his trip, the crowd gasped. He was mounting his horse from the wrong side!

At 3:45, the sky grew dark. Rain was on its way. Quickly, the horse and rider covered the short distance to the dock. Randall led the pony onto the riverboat. Just then, drops began to fall.

The paddle wheel turned. The *Antelope* moved north. Now Randall had several hours to rest.

As the boat neared Sacramento, the weather grew steadily worse. It was 2:00 in the morning when Randall jumped onto the dock. The regular Pony Express rider, Billy Hamilton, waited.

An express agent added the Sacramento mail to the saddlebag. And Hamilton mounted. There was no one to see him off in the heavy, dark rain.

The citizens of Sacramento were excited about the start of the Pony Express too. But they were not foolish enough to come out into a pouring rain in the middle of the night.

Hamilton spurred his horse and sped off on the soggy trail. He decided to go as fast as he could. The man who would take the mail from him was Warren Upson. He would face serious problems with the weather. He would have to climb over high mountains.

It's raining in the Sacramento Valley, Hamilton thought. So it must be snowing for Upson's ride in the high country. Maybe I can get to the relay station early. That will give Upson some extra time to plow his way through the snow.

Hamilton galloped past Fort Sutter. Gold had first been discovered there in 1849. Quickly, he sped along the American River to the relay station at Folsom. Here a new horse was saddled and ready for him. Hamilton found it  easy to dismount, throw the saddlebag onto the new horse, and remount in only two minutes.

He stopped four more times to change horses. And he made each stop as short as possible. He sped past Placerville. Finally as he rode into his final stop, Sportsman's Hall, he was proud. He'd beaten the schedule by 30 minutes.

Now it was Hamilton's turn to rest. He would not ride for the Pony again until the first delivery from St. Joseph arrived. It would be a wait of nine days. He'd stay here at Sportsman's Hall, his home station. Then he would gallop back the same 45 miles he had just come.

Hamilton had been the first one to carry the mail east from Sacramento. Now he would be the last one to carry letters west that had started in St. Joseph on April 3.

 25

Chapter

The Man with the Hardest Ride

Warren Upson loved the outdoors. He couldn't understand his father's life as an editor of the *Sacramento Union* newspaper. Why would his father want to spend his days at a desk?

Above all, Upson wanted to be with horses. He had learned to ride from Mexican *vaqueros*. They trained animals on the ranches near Sacramento. And Upson had ridden in a few rodeos.

Then Warren Upson saw the ad for Pony Express riders. He was sure the job was just right for him. Quickly, he signed up for an interview. His experience in the saddle and his eager answers impressed the representative sent by Russell, Majors, and Waddell.

But Upson had something else in his favor. He knew the high, winding trail across the Sierra Nevada from Sportsman's Hall, California, to Carson City, Nevada. He had ridden it many times in all kinds of weather. Besides, Warren Upson was thin and weighed no more than 125 pounds. He was just the size the company liked.

Upson got the job. As the second rider from the west, he would take the mail from Billy Hamilton and cross the Sierra Nevada.

On April 4, 1860, Upson was ready. Over and over, he paced the floor. He wished Billy Hamilton would arrive from Sacramento. Storm clouds were building over the mountains. A few flakes of snow were falling.

He patted his strong, stocky mustang. The animal was known for picking its way along rugged trails. This was the kind of horse Upson needed.

Upson wanted to get started. He would be lucky to cross the mountains in such weather. Many other men might have given up on the idea.

At last, he heard the sound of an approaching horse. Billy Hamilton burst into the station and tossed the mail to Upson.

Quickly, Upson spurred his horse. He rode out into the storm. But he didn't get far before he ran into trouble.

As the trail grew steep, he was forced to dismount and lead his horse. Upward they went. They climbed the slopes of the Sierra Nevada.

Upson struggled blindly. Everything was white. There was no way to make out the trail. He guessed the temperature was near zero. Wind and snow swirled around him. Ice formed on his eyelashes.

Upson rode short distances. Then he led the horse again. He struggled past snowdrifts higher than his head.

He was glad he had a daytime run. The company had planned it that way. His mountain trail was difficult enough in daylight. In the dark, it would be impossible.

Finally, he neared Strawberry Station, his first swing station. Upson chuckled as he pushed through the snow. Everyone knew there were no strawberries in these mountains. The station had been named that because the owner fed his horses straw. Then he charged the company for hay—at a much higher price.

Strawberry Station was snowed in. But a fresh horse was ready.

Upson changed horses in less than two minutes. Then he set out on foot. He led his fresh horse along the trail. He passed snowdrifts as high as 20 feet. Again he was not sure of the trail. So he mounted and trusted his horse.

Wind blew the snow. Horse and rider were lost in a sea of white. Any minute, they might slip over the edge of the trail. Or they might slide down into a canyon.

At Hope Valley, Upson again changed horses. He had come this way many times in better weather. Here and there, a snow-covered landmark looked familiar. And he knew the first part of his 85-mile trip would be the worst. He had to get over the last crest of the Sierra Nevada. Then the snow would be behind him.

How surprised the men tending the horses at the next two stations were! Just hours before, they'd been sure Upson couldn't possibly make his ride.

"This is a crazy plan to move the mail. It will never work," they had told each other. "And now we have this late snowstorm. No one expected it."

On the east side of the Sierra Nevada, Upson came out of the mountains. He was pleased to find himself on the well-worn wagon trail that so many pioneers had followed from the East.

He urged his horse to a gallop. His home station of Carson City lay just 14 miles ahead.

Later, he staggered from his horse. Warren Upson threw the precious saddlebag full of letters to the next rider, "Pony Bob" Haslam. Upson watched Haslam ride away to the east. Then he settled down for a much-needed rest.

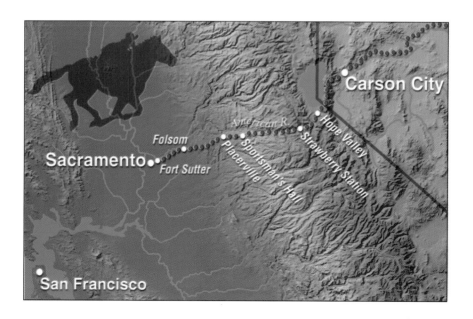

Chapter

Trouble Comes to the Pony Express

Americans were afraid war might come. It would be a war between the Northern states and the Southern states. And it would be a war about slavery.

But there was also a different kind of war—a war about land.

For years, new settlers had come from the East. They moved west into new lands. Some wanted gold and went to California. Others wanted land to farm.

Many times farmers cleared land and lived on it. But it was not theirs. It was Indian land.

Most Indians were friendly to the new settlers. To them, land was part of the earth. And the earth belonged to everyone.

When the white men came, the Indians shared the fish from the rivers. And they shared the deer and buffalo. For a long time, there was plenty to eat for everyone.

But more and more settlers came west. The Indians began to lose some of their lands. This made them angry. It made the Indian hunters worried. They were tired of having strangers invade their land.

The Indians who were the most angry and worried were the Paiutes. They lived in what are now the states of Utah and Nevada.

Rain had not come for a long time. The Paiutes watched their crops die in the fields. Then there was a long, cold winter. Many buffalo were killed by the settlers on the trail west. The Indian hunters could not find enough meat.

The partners who owned the Pony Express knew trouble might come at any time. They had rules for dealing with Indian tribes.

If you see one Indian, be friendly.
If there are three Indians, be careful.
If there are ten Indians, run.
Never shoot first.

The Pony Express had come to the West to make friends, not enemies. But now, the Paiutes were hungry, cold, and angry. Some of them had begun to raid the farmers and small towns. Would the Pony stations be next?

The Pony Express riders had made eight trips across the country. Now it was May. Bands of Paiutes were raiding against Utah stations. They stole food and horses. The Indians carried huge bows that sent their arrows flying. And many of them had rifles.

The Paiute chief was named *Numaga*. He wanted peace with the white men. He tried to stop the raids. But many of his men would not listen to him.

The raiding Indians stole Pony Express horses. Then they burned the stations. Sometimes they killed the men who took care of the horses. In three weeks, the Paiutes had killed 15 stationmasters.

The Indians killed one Pony Express rider too. He fell to the ground with an arrow in his back. But his brave horse galloped away. Following the path and with no rider, the animal delivered the mail to the next station.

Other tribes began to join the Paiutes. By June, members of the Sioux, Cheyenne, Shoshone, and Arapaho threatened riders along nearly 300 miles of the Pony Express trail.

An especially close call came to two station keepers at the Egan Canyon station. It was in what is now Nevada. They were Henry Wilson and his assistant, Albert Armstrong. One morning at breakfast, Indians surrounded their crude, one-room cabin.

Looking out the window, the two men saw a full band of Paiutes! Paint gleamed from their faces. Fierce cries filled the air.

Armstrong and Wilson grabbed their rifles. Keeping low, they fired through cracks in the cabin wall. But there were too many Indians for two men to hold off. The angry Indians kicked down the door and grabbed the two stationmasters. They tied Wilson and Armstrong hand and foot.

The Indians were hungry. And they saw breakfast on the table. Turning away from the tied men, they ate what was left on the table. Then they searched the storeroom for more food.

When they were finally full, they gathered sagebrush and firewood. They planned to burn the cabin and the two terrified white men with it.

Just then, a noise came from outside. Hoofbeats!

An army unit from a nearby fort had happened by. Quickly, their leader figured out what was happening inside.

About 20 soldiers burst into the cabin. Soon 18 Indians lay dead. The others rushed for the door and windows. They scrambled onto their ponies. In a moment, they were gone.

News of the Indian raids reached the Pony Express partners. The three men wondered what to do. They certainly didn't want any more people killed at their stations. But a 300-mile section of their Pony Express route was open to Indian attack. Nearly every day saw another station burned and another stationmaster killed.

The partners closed down the Pony Express. Mail delivery stopped for three weeks.

But without the mail delivery, the company could make no money. And they had already lost thousands of dollars' worth of stolen horses.

Now there was a new problem. Some of the riders were quitting. But William Russell was not willing to give up.

"We'll keep moving the mail," he promised his two partners. "And when we start again, we'll make two deliveries a week in each direction instead of one."

Majors and Waddell were stunned. How could that be done? And now Russell wanted to cut the price of a letter from $5 to $1! Could their company afford to stay in business?

Russell talked and talked. At last, he convinced his partners to trust him and his ideas. He was sure the Pony Express would return.

About that time, the United States Army sent troops into the Indian territory. The Paiutes and other tribes knew they could not fight against such force. They went back to their villages.

The Pony Express was back in business.

Chapter

Pony Bob Haslam and His Hard Ride

During the bad times with the Indians, several riders had narrow escapes from the Paiutes. But none of them came closer to danger than Robert Haslam.

Warren Upson continued to make his hard trip through the Sierra Nevada each week. When he came to Carson City, Nevada, he was always glad to see his relief rider waiting. That rider was 19-year-old Robert Haslam. He was called "Pony Bob" by his friends. It was Haslam's job to carry the mochila still closer to St. Joseph.

Indian trouble waited for Pony Bob around every turn, it seemed. His route was from Friday station to Bucklands, Nevada. It passed through the lands of the unhappy Paiutes. Peace with the Indians had always been a worry along this route.

The Paiutes had never been very friendly. Now they wanted to drive all the white men from their Utah and Nevada lands.

On May 11, 1860, Pony Bob took the mochila from Warren Upson. As usual, he spurred his horse and started east.

At first, there was no trouble. He changed to a fresh mount at each of his first three stations. Then Pony Bob came to the last station where he was to mount a fresh horse. He didn't find any animals there. The horses had been taken by settlers who needed them to fight raiding Indians.

Pony Bob had no choice. His tired mare would have to go on. He gave the horse some feed and water. Then he forced the weary animal on to his home station at Bucklands. This should have been Pony Bob's final stop.

He pulled the mochila from his saddle. Then he looked for his relief rider, Johnson Richardson. Soon he found the man. He was waiting inside the station. And he had drawn his pistol.

Richardson's face was white with fear. "There's no way I'm riding," he said. "I don't want to mess with those Indians."

The stationmaster, W. C. Marley, shook his head. "I can't talk him into going out there," he said. "Will you go on and make the next run? The company will pay you an extra $50."

Pony Bob decided that the mail must get through. And $50 was two weeks' salary. If Richardson didn't want the money, Pony Bob did. He grabbed the reins of a fresh horse. He threw the mochila across the saddle. Then he galloped eastward. Maybe high speed would keep the Indians well behind him.

After 35 miles, he came to the next swing station. He changed horses without trouble. After that he changed two more times.

Finally, he finished Richardson's run and passed the mochila to the next rider headed east, Jay Kelley.

Pony Bob's route should have been 75 miles. But that day he had traveled 190.

Haslam stretched out to sleep. He had just a few hours before the mochila from the east arrived. Then he would have to ride back west with it.

After a short rest, he was saddled up and headed west. His first station was Cold Springs. Everything had been peaceful there the day before.

Even before he rode into the yard, he knew there was trouble. The station had been burned. And the station keeper was dead.

There were no horses in sight. They had all been taken by the Indians.

Pony Bob gave his tired horse a drink. He knew the poor animal would have to go on.

At the next station, Sand Springs, he found the stock handler alone. Pony Bob sensed there were Indians nearby. Quickly, he talked the other man into going west with him.

The two men galloped along the trail. At the next station, 15 men had gathered to guard against Indian attack. They welcomed the two new men. They begged Pony Bob not to continue west.

"I haven't come all this way just to quit," he told them. After a short rest, he mounted a fresh horse and went on alone.

He finished Richardson's run without seeing any Indians. Then he rode his own route to the west.

When Pony Bob arrived at Friday station near Lake Tahoe, he finally dismounted. He had ridden 380 miles in 36 hours. He'd had almost no rest.

And he'd been in grave danger all the way.

Even with all his troubles, Haslam was nearly on schedule. The mail was running only three and one-half hours late.

But Pony Bob was not finished with his Indian troubles.

One day not long after his record ride, he rounded a bend on his horse. Suddenly, his path was blocked by 30 Paiutes with guns. There was no time to turn around and gallop away. He was already too close.

Not sure what to do, Pony Bob took out his revolver and rode at the Indians full speed. The surprised men suddenly parted to let Pony Bob pass between them.

As he spurred his horse, Bob heard the leader of the group shout, "You're a pretty good fellow!"

Pony Bob was never sure why the Indians let him pass. It may have been that they had heard about him—a fair and honest rider for the Pony Express.

Chapter 10

A Daring Bluff

Howard R. Egan was one of three Pony Express riders with the same last name. His run lay just west of Salt Lake City. Riding alone one night, he had a close call with a band of Paiutes.

Egan was riding through a canyon. As his horse moved down a hill, Egan saw the light of a campfire. It was a distance in front of him. In a few minutes, his worst fears came true. He was riding into a pass where Indians would be on both sides of him.

Egan slowed his horse. It was time to think carefully about what to do.

He could turn back and go north to another pass seven miles away. But that pass was likely to be guarded by Paiutes too.

Perhaps he should keep to the trail he was on. So far the Indians did not appear to have seen him.

While Egan was deciding what to do, he heard a dog bark. It had picked up his scent and was rushing down the hillside. It was making a great deal of noise.

There was no turning back now. Egan spurred his horse. He shot his pistol into the air. And he shouted at the top of his lungs.

The Indians heard all the noise. They thought a large number of men were coming through the pass. They looked about in confusion. Suddenly, Egan galloped his horse past them to safety.

Long after the Indian trouble was over, a friendly Paiute spoke to Egan. He said the Indians were curious about what the Pony Express riders carried in their cantinas. Was there magic in the pockets of the mochila?

Chapter 11

The Rider Who Would Not Die

Nick Wilson was 15 years old. He was a Mormon from the Utah territory. Wilson had lived with a Shoshone tribe as a boy. So he knew the ways of the Indians as well as any man.

He was eating dinner at Antelope station one night. Suddenly, he saw some Goshute Indians running off with the Pony Express horses. Wilson and the two stock handlers ran outside. They started after the thieves, who ran into a grove of cedars.

Wilson ran into the grove after them. The Indians quickly fitted arrows into their bows. Soon the air was thick with arrows. One of them struck Nick Wilson in the forehead. It was only two inches above his left eye.

The two stock handlers tried to remove the arrow. But it broke. They placed Wilson under a tree and escaped to the next station. They had left the young man for dead.

39

The next morning, the men returned to dig Wilson's grave. They were shocked to find him still alive. It took them all day to carry him to the nearest doctor.

The doctor removed the arrow. But he didn't expect Wilson to live. He told the other two men to keep a wet rag over the wound.

Six days later, the doctor was called back to treat Wilson again. He tried every kind of treatment he knew. For 12 more days, Wilson seemed close to death.

He did finally recover. The arrow had left a huge scar on his forehead. Nick Wilson never again removed his hat—not even to eat.

Chapter 12

Buffalo Bill and the Pony Express

William Frederick Cody was only 11 years old when his father died. He looked at the sad faces of his mother, his five sisters, and his baby brother. They would need a man in the family. Young William would be that man. He would have to get a job.

It was 1857. The family had moved from Iowa to Kansas two years before. Soon Bill was working an ox team for 50 cents a day. But he hoped for a better job.

In Kansas, wagon trains started west each week. They were put together and led by a freight company. It was owned by Russell, Majors, and Waddell. They were the same three men who would later own the Pony Express.

Young Billy Cody hurried to the company office. He knew it would be hard to get a job because of his age.

But the freight company had many people working for them. Maybe he could get some kind of a job there. He had to support his mother and the younger children.

Bill was a brave and friendly boy. He was soon hired as a messenger. The job paid $25 a month. It was his job to ride back and forth between the wagon trains headed along the trail to Utah. Plodding along on a mule, he carried messages for the company. Sometimes he took care of the livestock too.

After three years, Bill wanted a better and more exciting job. Each time he came near the office of Russell, Majors, and Waddell, he went inside to talk to Mr. Majors. Could he please be a rider for the new Pony Express? He was quick and brave. He was an excellent marksman with a gun. Couldn't he just be a substitute rider?

Each time, Mr. Majors shook his head. A Pony Express rider was supposed to be 18—or nearly that old. Bill was much too young.

But when Bill was 15, Mr. Majors gave in. He assigned the 100-pound boy a 45-mile run. It was in one of the most dangerous parts of the Pony Express route. Thieves and roughnecks often chased the riders.

Bill's boss was a man named Jack Slade. He was a tough frontiersman. Slade was not happy about his new young employee. But he soon saw how well young Cody could ride and shoot. And the boy was quick-witted. So he transferred Bill to a 116-mile stretch. This, too, was an area filled with outlaws and unfriendly Indians.

One day, Bill heard some news from another rider. Two dangerous men were on the trail ahead. They had tried to rob a stagecoach. But their horses had not been fast enough to catch it.

Now these men were somewhere ahead on the trail.

Bill knew there was a good deal of money in his mochila. He wondered if the outlaws knew about the money too. He needed a clever plan.

Bill placed the mochila with its money and letters across the saddle. Then he threw a second mochila on top of it. But this one was stuffed with worthless papers.

He set out on his way. Before long, he came to a narrow pass between the hills.

"Hands up!" a voice ordered. "Get down from that horse."

Bill did as he was told. Then he pretended to argue with the two men who had held him up. "I'm here on government business," Bill said.

But the bandits just laughed at him. They began to wave their pistols about. One of them threatened to shoot Bill.

"All right. All right," said Bill. He pulled the top mochila off the saddle. Then he threw it in the man's face. As the man struggled with the false mochila, Bill pulled out his gun and shot him in the shoulder. Then he scrambled onto his horse. By the time the second man could follow him, Bill had escaped with the real mochila filled with money and letters.

Bill Cody was not one of the first boys to ride for the company. And he was not there when the Pony ended. He was a Pony Express rider for only a few months during 1861. But even though he rode just a short time, the stories about him are well known because he later became very famous.

43

After his months with the Pony Express, Bill served as a Union scout in the Civil War. And he joined an antislavery group called the Jayhawks. For a time after the war, he worked on the construction of the railroad.

Then came the time when Bill earned a special nickname. He was given a contract by the government. It was his job to shoot the buffalo that roamed the plains. Buffalo meat was needed to feed the huge crews of men building the railroad.

Bill was a fine shot. The job was just the right one for him. In the year and a half he hunted buffalo for the U.S. government, he is said to have killed over 4,000 of the animals. Their meat fed hundreds of workers. Soon William Cody was known all over the West as "Buffalo Bill."

 44

Chapter 13

Wild Bill Hickok: A Man of the West

James Butler Hickok was born in Illinois. He moved to Kansas when he was 18. To support himself, he held a series of jobs. He was a farm worker, town constable, and stagecoach driver. He became known for his bravery and for his skill with a gun.

Hickok longed to be a Pony Express rider. But two things stood in his way. He was older than many of the men who worked for the Pony. And he stood 6 feet 1 inch tall. Even though thin, he weighed more than the 130-pound limit for riders.

Hickok was 24 when he went to work for the Pony. He had finally been hired as an assistant stockman at the Rock Creek station in Nebraska. It was his job to feed and water the horses and mules. He also did odd jobs around the station. Once in a while, another rider was sick. So he did have a chance to carry the mail.

Hickok was soon noticed because of his size and appearance. His light brown hair came to his shoulders. His mustache curled down to his chin. When he dressed up, he wore a fringed deerskin shirt and pants.

In time, trouble came to the Rock Creek station.

The land and log cabin had belonged to a man named David McCanles. He sold the property to the Pony Express. But the company was behind in its payments to him.

McCanles began to pester the station agent, Horace Wellman. Wellman explained each time. Payment had to come from the Pony Express company office. There was nothing he could do.

Again and again during the early summer of 1861, McCanles came to the agent. He became ruder and more demanding.

"Where's my money?" he growled. "Give it to me or you'll be sorry."

The men at the station hated and feared McCanles. They were afraid of his temper.

McCanles loved to tease Hickok because his upper lip stuck out over the lower one. Cruelly, McCanles called Hickok "Duck Bill."

One day in July, four horses trotted up to the Rock Creek station. On the first two rode David McCanles and his 12-year-old son, Monroe. The two other men were McCanles's brother, James, and a friend.

As usual, McCanles demanded his money from the frightened station agent. Then Hickok came into the room. Angry voices rose. A fight broke out.

When it was over, McCanles and the other two men were dead. The young boy had run away.

Hickok was arrested. Now his fame spread. Always good with a gun, he now earned the nickname "Wild Bill."

The McCanles boy testified that Hickok was a madman. He had shot the other three men without reason.

Wild Bill's friends were stunned. They insisted this could not be true. They knew Hickok as a man who would never attack unless his life was in danger.

After hearing all the evidence, the judge decided to let Hickok go. He held that Wild Bill had been "defending government property used to move the U.S. mail."

No one ever called him "Duck Bill" after that.

46

Chapter

The Pony's Fame Spreads

Not all those who used the services of the Pony Express were Americans. Some of them were businessmen in Europe. They had invested in the mining operations of Nevada, Colorado, and California. But it was hard to keep in touch with those operations.

The fame of the Pony spread. These investors read stories in British and French newspapers. This Pony Express was exciting. Now they saw a way to communicate with their offices in the American West.

The British government went even further. It held vast lands in the Far East. These lands were on the other side of the Pacific Ocean. Officials began sending messages by ship from England to New York. Then the information was telegraphed from New York to St. Joseph. The Pony Express raced it to Sacramento.

Again the telegraph was used. It sent the information from Sacramento to San Francisco. From there, the messages were carried by ship to the Orient. As difficult as such a route might seem, it was actually faster than sending information by ship from England to the Orient.

Chapter

The Daring Rides Continue

Thomas Owen King once rode 80 miles when he was very tired. When he arrived at his next station, he reported that he had not passed Henry Worley. Worley was the rider from the other direction.

King later told his friends, "Worley reported the same thing about me at the other station. We had both been sound asleep in our saddles. We never knew we had passed each other."

Rider **William Campbell** had a big surprise one night. Riding his route in the dark, he came upon a pack of wolves. They were feeding on a dead horse. Campbell galloped by. But some of the wolves took off after him. Campbell did not have his gun. He feared his horse would be killed. So he pulled out the horn he blew to let stationmasters know he was near. Each time the wolves got near, Campbell blew a mighty blast on the horn. This seemed to slow the wolves down for a few minutes. At last, Campbell and his horse made it safely to the next station.

A few months later, Campbell was the rider who carried the text of Abraham Lincoln's inaugural address into California in the fastest Pony Express time ever—7 days 17 hours.

Jim Moore's famous ride was a result of outlaws, not Indians. Moore was to carry important government papers. He began his 140-mile run from Midway station, Nebraska. It stretched to Julesburg, Colorado. Moore arrived at the log cabin express station. But he found the next rider to head east had been murdered. So Moore turned and started back over the trail he had just covered. When he finished, he had covered 280 miles in less than 15 hours. That was an average of 18 miles an hour. It was probably the fastest speed record of any one Pony Express rider.

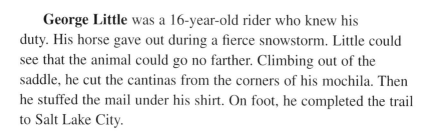

George Little was a 16-year-old rider who knew his duty. His horse gave out during a fierce snowstorm. Little could see that the animal could go no farther. Climbing out of the saddle, he cut the cantinas from the corners of his mochila. Then he stuffed the mail under his shirt. On foot, he completed the trail to Salt Lake City.

Chapter

The Beginning of the End

All through the spring and summer of 1861, the Pony Express continued to lose money. Congress had never voted Russell, Majors, and Waddell the contract they had been so sure of. Their other shipping businesses made money. But there was never enough to make up for the losses of the Pony.

Much of the problem was the approach of the Civil War. Northern senators and Southern senators in Congress argued endlessly. No one would agree on any issue. Several times, a bill came before Congress to pay the Pony Express. But there were never enough votes.

The Southern congressmen wanted all the money to go to the Butterfield Stage Company. That company had its route deep in the South. If war came, the Southern states might be able to capture that Butterfield route.

Every bill that would have helped the Pony failed. And its greatest supporter, Senator Gwin, had lost much of his power in the government.

Then something happened that has never been explained. William Russell and another man were accused of a crime. Three million dollars had disappeared from a government bank account. The money was supposed to be used for Indian affairs.

Russell had $387,000 in his own bank account. The authorities claimed it was part of the missing money. They arrested him.

Russell was never convicted of any crime. But his good name had been ruined. He resigned from the Pony Express.

The start of war came closer and closer. In February 1861, the government ordered the Butterfield and Wells Fargo Companies to move their stagecoach routes north. They were also ordered to merge with the Pony Express.

The Pony still sent out single horses and riders. But now they were used on shorter and shorter routes.

Then came the final blow.

Work gangs were racing to finish the telegraph line from coast to coast. Over 40,000 wooden poles went into the ground. Miles of wire were strung between them.

As the miles of telegraph spread, the routes where the Pony Express was needed grew shorter. Wires could carry the words. So why did anyone need a horse and rider?

On October 24, 1861, the two ends of the telegraph line were connected in Salt Lake City.

Riders galloping into their home stations heard the news. "They don't need us boys any more," they told one another.

Two days later, the Pony Express ended its service.

 52

Chapter 17

The Later Years

The riders of the Pony Express were brave. And they took many risks. Their job was exciting. But, at the same time, it could be the loneliest work in the world.

All were young when they rode for the Pony. So they went on to other work. During the 19 months the company was in business, nearly 200 young men rode at one time or another. Toward the end, the men were very young. Here is what is known about the later lives of some of them.

Buffalo Bill Cody became famous as an entertainer with his "Buffalo Bill's Wild West Show." Crowds from all over America and Europe rushed to see his performances. Books were written about this famous frontiersman. And he met many important people.

Some of the stories Buffalo Bill told about his frontier days may not be entirely true. He could spend hours talking about his miracle escapes from highwaymen and Indians.

Many years after he left the Pony Express, he claimed to have made the longest nonstop ride in the history of the company. He claimed to have ridden four miles farther than Pony Bob Haslam. No records remain to prove whether this was true.

In 1894, Buffalo Bill retired from show business. He moved to a ranch in Wyoming. There he lived peacefully until his death in 1917. He was 69.

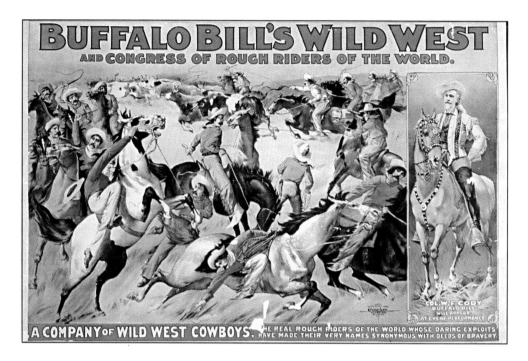

BUFFALO BILL'S WILD WEST AND CONGRESS OF ROUGH RIDERS OF THE WORLD. A COMPANY OF WILD WEST COWBOYS. THE REAL ROUGH RIDERS OF THE WORLD WHOSE DARING EXPLOITS HAVE MADE THEIR VERY NAMES SYNONYMOUS WITH DEEDS OF BRAVERY. COL. W. F. CODY BUFFALO BILL WILL APPEAR AT EVERY PERFORMANCE

Like Buffalo Bill, **Wild Bill Hickok** left the Pony Express in the spring of 1861. His great courage and skill with a gun earned him a job as a scout for the Union army. After the war, he scouted Indians for General George Custer.

Buffalo Bill Cody invited his old friend Hickok to join him in show business. Wild Bill appeared with Cody for a short time in 1872. But he was not a showman. He soon retired quietly to a small ranch.

In 1876, Hickok was shot to death while playing cards in a saloon in the Dakota territory. He was 39 years old.

Warren Upson quit his job with the Pony Express in the spring of 1861. He had no wish to work for the new management.

Handsome **Johnny Fry,** the first rider from St. Joseph, continued to charm the young ladies. He was one of the few who stayed with the company the full 19 months. When the Civil War began, he signed up with the Union forces. Before long, he was killed in battle.

Pony Bob Haslam was another man who worked for the Pony Express the entire 19 months. Later he rode for Wells Fargo. He was famous for his ability to race a horse faster than anyone who challenged him. In later years, he served as a U.S. deputy marshal in Salt Lake City.

Richard Egan's run stretched from Salt Lake City to Rush Valley. He is the best known of the Mormon riders. He and three other Pony Express men later became bishops in the church.

David Jay began riding for the Pony at age 13. He lived to be 83.

Another rider, **Bill Campbell**, sold mules to the government after the war. Later, he became a state senator in Nebraska.

Nick Wilson, the 15-year-old who was shot in the forehead with an arrow, lived to be 71.

"Bronco Charlie" Miller was only 11 when he rode for the company during its last five months. Miller lived to be 105. He died in 1955. He was the last Pony Express rider to die.

In all, the riders of the Pony Express traveled more than 600,000 miles. They carried almost 35,000 pieces of mail. They helped Americans reach out to one another through letters. And they united the East and the West to make our nation strong.

They lived a period in history like no other.

Index